Dolphins

Library of Congress Number: 87-28717

1 2 3 4 5 6 7 8 9 0   91 90 89 88 87

Printed and bound in the United States of America.

Library of Congress Cataloging in Publication Data

Dolphins.

   (Science and its secrets)
   Includes index.
   Summary: Discusses dolphins in the wild and in captivity,
their physical and mental capabilities, and their relationship
with man.
   1. Dolphins—Juvenile literature.   [1. Dolphins]
I. Series.
QL737.C432D66   1988   599.5'3   87-28717
ISBN 0-8172-3085-8 (lib. bdg.)
ISBN 0-8172-3091-2 (softcover)

DOLPHINS

🌳 Raintree Publishers — Milwaukee

Contents

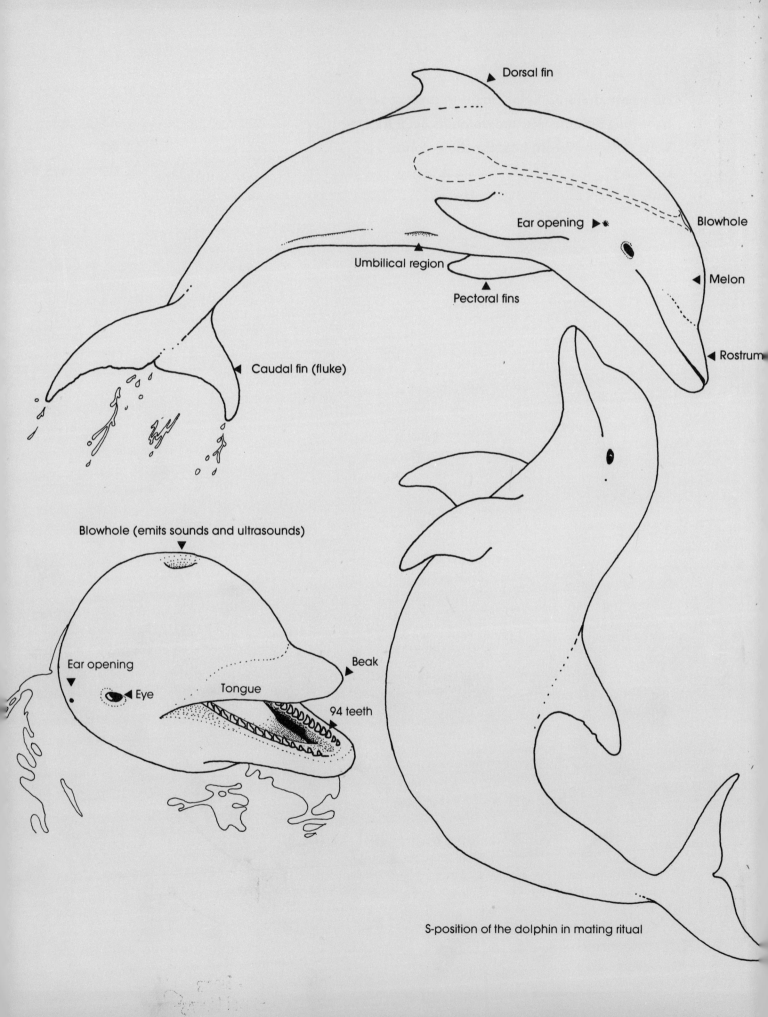

Dorsal fin

Ear opening ▶ ✳

Blowhole

Melon

Rostrum

Umbilical region

Pectoral fins

Caudal fin (fluke)

Blowhole (emits sounds and ultrasounds)

Ear opening

Eye

Beak

Tongue

94 teeth

S-position of the dolphin in mating ritual

Who is the dolphin?

The dolphin is a small, whale-like animal. It lives in all of the oceans and in some rivers. The dolphin looks like a fish, but it is actually a mammal. Therefore, it breathes air and not water. Dolphins belong to an order of mammals called cetaceans (pronounced see TAY shuhnz). This name comes from a Latin word meaning "large sea animal." Cetaceans are especially well-suited to life in the sea. There are over one hundred different animals in this order. It includes animals such as whales, sperm whales, and porpoises. The largest member of this order is the blue whale. It can grow 98 feet (30 meters) long. The killer whale is also part of this order. In fact, it is one of the dolphin's closest relatives. It is also one of the dolphin's enemies.

The dolphin is a social animal. Social animals live together in groups and depend on one another for survival. The dolphin is also an unusually friendly animal. It needs the company of others. It is especially fond of people and other dolphins. The dolphin is also known to be very intelligent. It may be the most intelligent animal after the human being.

Why is the dolphin so interesting?

It is a scorching afternoon in July. The sea is as smooth as a millpond. A single small boat is pushed by its outboard motor toward land. The bluish mountains of Corsica are blurred by the warm mist rising from the sea.

A girl with darkly tanned skin sleeps lazily on the deck of the boat. From time to time she wakes to glance at the waveless sea. It is a likely area for a meeting with dolphins. It is also a good spot to see black masses of whales emerge. These creatures are a little frightening. But like the dolphins, they are not dangerous.

Suddenly, a wave disturbs the peaceful waters. A smooth, dark flipper shoots out of the water. In a moment, it disappears again. Soon afterwards, dark round backs can be seen at the water's surface. The dolphins have arrived! Their dark shadows can be seen circling the boat and diving beneath the hull. On board, everyone is filled with excitement.

For the next half an hour, the dolphins playfully follow the sail-

boat. Or, rather, the sailboat follows them. To the dolphins, it is all a big game. They leap, alone or in pairs. Mothers with their little dolphins, or small groups of three or four, splash about in the water. Some dive in and out under the boat, suddenly poking up toward the surface. Others swim beside the boat with slow, powerful wave-like motions of their tail flippers. Sometimes the dolphins lie on

The dolphin's shape makes it a quick, graceful swimmer. But it is also very powerful. Its sharp turns, sudden stops, and high jumps make it entertaining to watch.

their sides. In this position, they can use their sharp little eyes to watch the people on board. They can also watch the speeding boat. But what a joke! The speedboat travels a mere five knots. The dolphins, however, can swim at

7

A meeting with dolphins in the wild is an exciting occasion. It is also rare. Here, the girl's foot gently touches the dolphin's back. The dolphin was not frightened by the girl's touch and returned several times.

about thirty knots with very little effort. (A knot is a measurement used by sailors. A car's speed is given in miles per hour; a boat's speed is measured in knots. One knot is one nautical mile per hour).

In front of the bow, the dolphins put on a splendid underwater show. They move as if directed by an invisible master. With unbelievable accuracy, they create perfect geometric figures in the water. One small, daring dolphin rubs itself against the bow of the boat. Then, as part of its play, it plows through the rolling water at the bow. On board, the girl notices this game. She walks to the far end of the sailboat and tries to touch the dolphin's back with her toes. The dolphin swerves away from the girl's foot. Then, amazingly, the dolphin swims up close again. Several times the girl touches it for a few seconds.

It is an exciting moment. What is it that draws the dolphins to people? In the same way, what is it that draws people to dolphins? The girl is not thinking about what a unique experience she is having. The same is true, of course, for the dolphins. But something is happening. This is a meeting whose origins go back to the beginning of time. It goes back to an era in which the dolphins' ancestors lived on land. For that is where dolphins once lived before making their way to the water. By a slow process of change, called evolution, the dolphin is now a water animal. It is one of many scientific mysteries that people may never fully understand.

The game goes on for at least two minutes. But like everything else, this, too, has to end. The friendly dolphin finally moves away. As it does, it leaps up as if to take one final bow. Suddenly, the surface of the sea is calm again.

How can people learn more about the dolphin?

For most people, it is not possible to study dolphins in the wild. Meetings such as the one described above are rare. Even for scientists, it is difficult to study dolphins in the wild. For this reason, scientists try to recreate the dolphins' environment where they can study them. An animal's environment is its home. It includes the conditions and surroundings in which that animal is naturally found. These re-created environments are known as zoos. Some zoos are specifically for marine animals, such as the dolphin. These are called marine zoos. You may have visited a place like this.

One of the most famous of these zoos is Marineland of Antibes. This Marineland is found in France between the cities of Antibes and Nice. It is the largest European open-air marine zoo. Marine zoos like this one can also be found in many parts of the United States. Warmer areas such as California and Florida are especially good locations. The temperatures of these states are fairly warm year round. Warm temperatures are important for dolphins, which are often found in tropical waters. Extremely cold temperatures would not be good for them.

Many marine zoos put on dolphin shows daily. Depending on the location, some zoos may only have shows at certain times of the year. At the time of this writing, two very special dolphins, named Splash and Lucky, were the stars of Marineland's show. These two dolphins were captured together in the Caribbean Sea.

Their jumps are, without question, the most spectacular part of the show. The dolphins use them to show their physical strength. With speed and grace, Splash can shoot himself 16 feet (5 m) into the air. The dolphin's powerful tail flipper allows it to climb to heights like this.

The dolphin's jumps are a sort of artwork. Dolphins move very beautifully. A trip to a marine zoo gives people the chance to see this for themselves. At the zoo, people get a close-up view of dolphins. If not for the zoos, few people would ever have the chance to see a live dolphin. In Europe, Marineland can even offer open air shows.

For this trick, a ball is placed at the end of a long pole. The ball sits 10 feet (3 m) above the water's surface. The dolphins must jump several feet into the air to reach it. They hit the target each time without fail.

Why must dolphins be captured?

Studying dolphins in the wild is very hard. To study them up close, scientists capture dolphins from the sea. They are then kept in marine zoos and other places like this. At present, this is the most successful way to study the dolphin and its behavior.

Some people do not agree with this method. The great marine explorer, Jacques Cousteau, is one such person. Cousteau says that the study of captured dolphins is a study of "denatured and perverted" animals. In other words, he suggests that dolphins in zoos do not act naturally. This means that captive dolphins are different from dolphins in the wild.

But studies of dolphins in the wild are not nearly as successful. Cousteau and the crew of his boat, the *Calypso,* tried to study dolphins in the wild. In twenty-five years, they were only able to approach the same dolphin group twice. The results of their studies were limited. So marine zoos are worthwhile. Also, the shows at the zoos can earn a lot of money. This money can be used to pay for different research projects.

But where are dolphins caught, and how do people catch them? Many dolphins are found in the open sea near Florida. Large groups of them are often spotted close to the coast. They are rarely spotted more than five hundred miles out. A person trying to catch dolphins uses fairly large boats. These boats are equipped to handle ma-

rine animals. But dolphins must be given special care.

The boat crews skillfully use their nets to surround some of the dolphins. As soon as it feels caught and unable to escape, the dolphin becomes calm. When the dolphins are calm, some of the crew members dive down to look at the dolphins. They then choose those they want to keep. A sick or wounded animal is let go at once. Females about to give birth are also sent back to the sea. The first few days of captivity are hard on an animal. These dolphins would not survive the stress. Catching dolphins is hard work. It requires true experts. Great care must be taken not to hurt the animals. The capture and sale of dolphins is strictly controlled in the United States. It has been for a long time.

After certain dolphins are chosen, they must be lifted onto the boats. Each dolphin is placed in a

These dolphins surface to take a fresh breath of air.

Hammocks like these are used to transport dolphins.

hammock made of thick canvas. The hammock has slots for the flippers, and the tail hangs out the back. In Florida, the trip back is not really a problem. The capture is made very close to the coasts. From there, the dolphin is quickly put into a pool. There it will be able to swim again. This is very important for the dolphin's survival.

But some trips are not so easy. Sometimes the animal must be taken across the Atlantic Ocean. This causes some extra problems. Dolphins have very fragile skin. The scientists know this. They coat the dolphin with a thick layer of grease to further protect it. Special care is taken around the eyes and the blowhole. The blowhole is a small opening on the dolphin's head through which it breathes. Even the powerful tail fin must be handled carefully. This fin, called the caudal fin, is fragile out of the water.

When the dolphin is put back in the water, the scientists will then need to watch the animal. A dolphin gets stiff after not moving for a long time. It can lose its sense of balance and fall over on its back. In this position, it is in danger. It could drown because its blowhole is in the water.

Capture attempts have been made in the Mediterranean. The dolphin found in this area is the common dolphin. Its scientific name is *Delphinus delphis*. The common dolphin is much more shy than its cousin, the bottle-nosed dolphin. And it is not nearly as hardy. A common dolphin has never been able to survive the shock of capture.

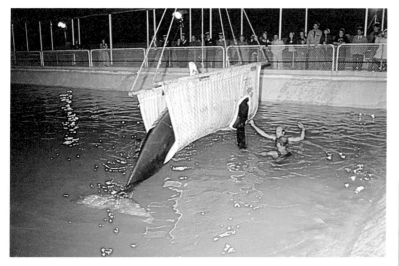

This dolphin has traveled far from the ocean. Here it is being lowered into the pool of a marine zoo (left).

Placing the dolphin into the water is an exciting moment (below left).

After not moving, the dolphin may be stiff. The numbness could cause the dolphin to lose its balance. It could drown if its blowhole is not kept out of the water.

How is a dolphin born?

Dolphins are very rarely born in captivity. This is true of many animals. Many animals simply do not mate, or breed, well out of their environments. But from their studies, scientists now have a better understanding of the process. Much of their information comes from what they see in their aquariums. Some is gained from scientists' work in other countries.

A group, or school, of dolphins swims in the warm waters of the Caribbean Sea. Their gray backs show at the surface from time to time. They are moving very fast. Under water, the picture is almost magical. The large, dark groups of males circle three females. One of the females seems to be in trouble. Now and then, her whole body shakes violently, or shudders. With each shudder, the other two females come nearer to her.

Dolphins spend much of their time at play. Play is an important part of their behavior. Like humans, the dolphins' behavior also seems to have a code. Young dolphins learn this code from their parents.

Before long, a small tail appears near the base of the female's tail. A small amount of blood floats in the water. Now there are more shakes. Then suddenly, a small chocolate-brown object is pushed from the female's body. The spindle-shaped object is a completely formed baby dolphin. The baby dolphin must breathe immediately or die. Sometimes a newborn dolphin does not react at once. The other dolphins then take charge of it. They will push it toward the surface. There it will take its first gulp of air. The newborn dolphin is a bit dazed. All the commotion and the dazzling light confuse it. The family fusses around and watches it. Some help it in its first acts of life. The big-muscled males continue to circle the mother and her baby. They are ready to defend the group against any possible attack. Sharks are often attracted by the mother's blood. The baby dolphin also attracts them. Right after birth, it is a powerless, clumsy animal. The males will protect it while it gains strength.

During the time of a birth, each member of the dolphin community has a job to do. Each will do its job properly. First, the females will assist the mother. After that, they help the newborn in its first moments of life. After that, the males take charge. The group has been weakened and distracted by the birth of the baby. The males will protect them until all is back to normal.

Although it is rare, a dolphin can be born in captivity. One example of this took place off Malaga. There, some fishermen accidentally captured a dolphin in their nets. The dolphin was quickly shipped to the Marineland Zoo. The dolphin, a large female, was named Evelyne. She weighed 660 pounds (300 kg) and now leads a peaceful existence.

From the beginning, Evelyne refused all training. But she liked to play with another dolphin named Stanley. Both Evelyne and Stanley were the same kind, or species, of dolphin. They were of the *Tursiops* species. This kind of dolphin is commonly known as the bottle-nosed dolphin. This is the best known kind of dolphin. It is the bottle-nosed dolphins that often perform in the zoos.

The dolphins' trainer, Martin Paddley, noticed how well Evelyne and Stanley got along. He hoped that their games might lead to something bigger. Just maybe, the dolphins would mate.

Paddley's dream of a birth in captivity came true. It happened on the morning of June 26, 1979. That morning, one of the trainers noticed something strange in the pool. Many of the animals seemed nervous. Even the killer whales, Kim and Betty, seemed jumpy. Evelyne, in one corner, was moving in a strange way. To the trainer's amazement, a little dolphin suddenly appeared. Dolphins are born tail first so that they do not drown. After they come from the mother's body, the young must be pushed to the surface to breathe.

A baby dolphin's first feeding is somewhat slow. It takes the newborn a little while to figure things out. At first, a lot of milk is wasted.

What milk the baby does not drink ends up in the water. In the ocean, other female dolphins help the baby. They teach the newborn to feed by pushing it toward its mother's nipples. The female dolphin has two nipples. Special muscles around each nipple force the milk into the baby's mouth. In this way, the baby dolphin does not have to suck. The dolphin's milk is also very thick. This keeps it from getting too watered down by the seawater. The mother dolphin makes feeding even easier by rolling slightly to the side. Soon, the newborn understands. It will cling to its mother's nipple for a full meal. It may take its mother's milk for as long as eighteen months.

A dolphin usually has only one baby. Twins are very rare. A baby dolphin is very large for a newborn. It is already a third of its mother's length. It also looks very much like an adult dolphin. It will not change much in appearance as it grows. As you know, dolphins are mammals. Because of this, baby dolphins develop inside their mother. It takes eleven or twelve months for a baby dolphin to fully develop. Birth takes place on or close to the surface. The baby does not have to go far for its first breath. After that, the baby dolphin explores its mother's body. It gently touches her with its rostrum. In this way, it will always know her from other members of the school.

Only a day after its birth, the baby dolphin swims beside its mother. Dolphins are fully formed at birth. Baby dolphins may take milk from their mothers for almost two years.

13

What is known about the dolphins' mating habits?

Dolphins spend a lot of time playing. Some of their play is actually part of their mating process. They are known to do this even before they are able to have young. In fact, this love play takes up a large part of the dolphin's life. This is even more true in captivity. There, males and females are always together. In the wild, they are not. In their natural environment, dolphins live in larger spaces.

But in the zoos and other aquariums, the dolphins are always near each other. They are always touching, patting, or even playing

Dolphins are usually very sociable animals. But a dolphin can also easily amuse itself. A ball or other floating object will hold the dolphin's attention for hours.

roughly. As adults, the play turns to mating. The male dolphin usually begins the mating process. Attracted to the females, he timidly approaches one. He circles her, hesitates, and then swims away. On his next pass, he gently brushes against her. If he is not pushed away, he rubs himself against her. Then he holds himself in an S-position for several seconds. Dolphin experts know this as a sign of his feelings.

In the next weeks, the male and female dolphins are together more and more. In fact, they do not leave each other anymore. They swim together, teasing, poking, and nibbling at each other. Sometimes the dolphins' mating games are very beautiful. The animals seem to dance as they

twist, turn, jump, splash, and swim gracefully side by side. In many ways, their mating becomes a ballet of love. They finally come together belly to belly. Mating takes place near the water's surface. It often lasts no longer than thirty seconds.

Many marine zoos have aquariums or observation rooms. From there, scientists can study the mating process first hand.

What do dolphins eat?

At birth, a dolphin weighs about 55 pounds (25 kg). It feeds on its mother's milk until it is almost two years old. After that, it begins to eat fish. By the age of five or six, the dolphin reaches its adult length and weight. Its adult weight is about 385 to 440 pounds (175 to 200 kg). The dolphin must eat 13 to 14 pounds (6 to 7 kg) of fish per day to reach this weight. In the winter, a dolphin eats even more. Then it may eat about 22 pounds (10 kg) of fish per day. Of course, larger dolphins need even more food. Some very powerful dolphins eat up to 33 pounds (15 kg).

In the ocean, dolphins are much more active. There are also times when food is hard to find. For both reasons, wild dolphins eat much more food. A thick layer of fat then forms over the dolphin's body. This gives the dolphin an extra source of energy. This layer of fat, called blubber, has another

use. It keeps the dolphin warm. The dolphin, like man, is a warm-blooded animal. Its blood must be kept at a certain temperature. Blubber protects the dolphin during deep, cold dives.

Dolphins usually feed on fish near the surface. They will also eat squid and crustaceans. Crustaceans are hard-shelled animals like lobsters and crabs. Dolphins swallow their food whole. They use their teeth only to catch and hold their prey.

One of the dolphin's favorite foods is a fish called mullet. To catch mullets, dolphins actually herd them like cattle. Coming upon a school of mullets, the dolphins chase them toward shallow coastal waters. This often happens along the Atlantic coast of Mauritania, a country in northern Africa. The frightened fish end up trapped against the beaches. The dolphins then eat a bellyfull of them. This feeding method also helps the people living on the coasts. These people, called Imragens, watch for the dolphins to come. Then they take their nets into the water. They catch the mullets that the dolphins drive toward shore.

The dolphin's eating habits are very efficient. In only a few years, they change the fragile baby dolphin into a sleek, powerful adult.

Fish like mackerel and herring are enough to bring good health to the dolphin. But it is important that the fish are very fresh.

Here, a dolphin and a killer whale sing for their supper. Dolphins make a whole range of noises. Their sounds include clicks, whistles, quacks, bleats, and squawks.

Does the dolphin really smile?

The dolphin may be one of the most best-loved of all animals. Its wide, toothy grin easily wins over and amuses many people. This is especially true of the bottle-nosed dolphin. This dolphin is the well-known star of many marine zoos. It is easier to train this dolphin than any other kind. For one thing, it adapts well. That means it easily adjusts to new environments or situations. It is very hard for some animals to live in a cage. But the bottle-nosed can adapt to these living conditions. This makes it a good dolphin to use in training and scientific studies.

But does the dolphin really smile? No, it does not really. Dolphins just seem to be smiling. The shape of the dolphin's head and of the beak, or rostrum, causes this grin. The front of the dolphin's head rises sharply, like a bump. This rise is caused by a fatty organ called the melon. Where the melon and the rostrum meet, the dolphin's jaws curl up as if in a smile. The little, wrinkled eyes add to this look. In people's imaginations, the dolphin really is smiling. They are drawn to the dolphin's pleasant face.

People are definitely fond of the dolphin. Its smiling face and friendly nature are reason enough alone. But on top of this, the dolphin is also one of the most intelligent animals. Many people, including scientists, find this an interesting feature.

Tursiops truncatus is more commonly known as the bottle-nosed dolphin. It is the most domestic of all dolphins.

The dolphin's winning "smile" is not really a smile at all. The dolphin just seems to smile because of the shape of its head and beak. The animal's friendly nature makes the smile seem all the more fitting.

This young woman is a trainer at the Flipper Sea School in Florida. Her sign asks you not to confuse the dolphin with the dolphin fish. The dolphin fish (on the right) is a large game fish. It is found in the warm salt waters of the Bahamas.

How does the dolphin swim?

People have been interested in dolphins for a very long time. This statue from the Museum of Archaeology in Athens, Greece, proves this. Dolphin-like figures circle it. Notice how their swimming movements have been exaggerated.

The dolphin's skin is the key to its speed. The skin's close-set folds move constantly as the dolphin swims. These movements fight the water's slowing effects.

The dolphin has a hairless, torpedo-shaped body. Its color ranges from light gray to black. Its back is darker than its belly. The dolphin's shape allows it to move easily in the water. It can travel in all positions: on its belly, on its back, or on its side. It can make sharp turns without slowing down. It can also make quick stops and jump to great heights.

The dolphin is a swift swimmer. Over long distances, it swims about 22 miles (35 km) per hour and does not seem to tire. In short bursts it can reach speeds of 30 miles (50 km) per hour. But some scientists think it can do much more.

For a long time, the dolphin's speed puzzled experts. From studies of the dolphin's size and shape, they estimated its speed. But their answer fell short of what the animal can actually do. The dolphin travels much faster than they expected. This mystery has not yet been solved. But two of the dolphin's major features may help explain this.

The first feature is the dolphin's powerful tail. Unlike fish, the dolphin has a horizontal tail. It is called a fluke. Dolphins move, or propel, themselves through the water with their flukes. As the fluke moves up and down, the animal is pushed forward. The flippers and dorsal, or back, fin are used for steering and balance.

The dolphin's second important feature is its skin. The dolphin's skin has many interesting qualities. Have you ever touched a dolphin's skin? If so, you probably remember how smooth it felt. The dolphin's skin has a sort of silky, soft feel to it.

In fact, the real secret of the dolphin's speed is the tiny movements of its skin. The dolphin's skin is formed of small, very close-set folds. These folds are constantly moving. They prevent the slowing effects of the water. Think about the last time you went swimming. Do you remember feeling the force of the water against you as you swam? This force is called a drag. As any body passes through water, little swirls of water form along the body's surface. These swirls create drag, which slows the body's speed. But the movement of the dolphin's skin stops these swirls from forming. The water surrounding the dolphin, then, is always very calm. This helps it swim very fast.

How deep can the dolphin dive?

This skull of a killer whale shows the teeth of this large marine animal. Killer whales have from forty to forty-eight teeth.

Dolphins spend much time on or near the water's surface. But their diving abilities impress researchers. Dolphins often swim at a depth of 100 to 150 feet (30 to 46 m). But no one knows exactly how deep they can go. There is some evidence that dolphins may be able to dive to 2,000 feet (610 m).

In normal weather, dolphins find food close to the surface. Then there is no need to search deep down. Now and then, dolphins do dive deeper. They dive and surface very quickly. They do not seem to have the pressure problems that human divers have. Human divers must not come to the surface too quickly. Surfacing too quickly can cause a painful condition known as the bends. The bends happen when bubbles of nitrogen gas form in a diver's bloodstream. These bubbles actually get stuck in the diver's joints. When a diver rises slowly, the bubbles do not form. The bends can cause terrible pain or even death. Dolphins are not bothered by this.

How do dolphins defend themselves?

Dolphins defend themselves with their jaws. The large bottle-nosed dolphin has jaws that have eighty to one hundred teeth. These teeth are cone-shaped and very sharp. But they are used only to catch and hold the dolphin's food. Food is swallowed whole.

Not all cetaceans have teeth. The order is divided into two groups: the toothed whales, and baleen whales. Baleen whales have no teeth. Instead, they have hundreds of thin plates in their mouths called baleen. Baleen whales feed mainly on plankton—drifting masses of tiny plants and animals. The dolphin, however, belongs to the toothed whale group.

Like many animals of this group, the dolphin has powerful jaws. They make a frightening weapon. Backed by great strength, the dolphin's jaws can be used for ramming. Dolphins are known to ram sharks trying to attack a member of the school.

Dolphins take short naps throughout the day. Females sleep at the surface. That way, their blowholes are kept out of the water. Males sleep below the surface. They rise now and then to take in fresh air.

Are there many kinds of dolphins?

There are many different types of dolphins. The bottle-nosed dolphin is the best known. But there are others.

The Amazon River dolphin is often found in the Amazon and other rivers of South America. Its beak is much longer than that of the bottle-nosed dolphin. It also has a small dorsal fin.

The beluga is another member of the dolphin family. It is a large dolphin and can grow up to 15 feet (5 m) long. It is a strange looking animal. It has a plump body and a small, rounded head. Its rostrum is short and flat. The beluga is extremely rare in captivity. But it can be trained just like the bottle-nosed dolphin.

The Risso's dolphin has a rounded head and no beak. It is easily spotted by its creased forehead. This crease runs from the animal's blowhole to its upper lip. The dolphin's lower jaw has six to fourteen teeth. The upper jaw has none.

The pilot whale is one of the largest members of the dolphin family. A layer of fat gives this dolphin a strange, round head. This fat contains a valuable oil, known as "blackfish-melon oil." The pilot whale can grow up to 28 feet (8 m) long and weigh in at three tons. Pilot whales commonly live in large groups called pods. Sometimes hundreds follow one or more leaders.

The white-sided dolphin of the Pacific Ocean is a high-spirited animal. This dolphin is a particularly strong swimmer. But it is best known for its jumping. The white-sided dolphin can jump to a height of 21 feet (6.5 m).

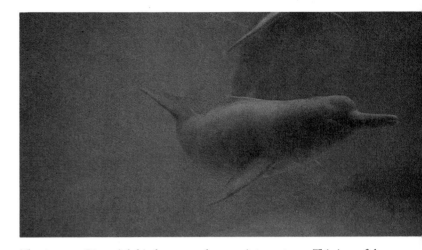

The Amazon River dolphin has a very long, pointy rostrum. This is useful for digging on the river bottoms, where it searches for food. This dolphin is found in the rivers of South America.

The beluga is a large, strange looking member of the dolphin family.

Scientists at Marineland of Antibes try to save a sickly Risso's dolphin.

The bottle-nosed dolphin has a mischievous looking eye which misses nothing.

Finally, there is the common dolphin. The common dolphin can be found in all oceans. Stories of these dolphins have been told for hundreds of years. They were heroes of many Greek and Roman myths and legends. Because of this, the common dolphin was sometimes honored in the temples. However, this dolphin does not live well in captivity.

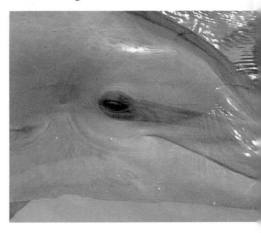

Does the dolphin have good eyesight?

Here, an Amazon River dolphin swims in water like that of its natural environment. The water is dark and cloudy. It is hard to see very far. This is what dolphins living in the Amazon, Orinoco, Ganges, and Indus rivers face.

The dolphin seems to play using its excellent eyesight. Its eyes, situated on opposite sides of its head, are very mobile. They can look in all directions, even toward the back. But eyesight alone does not explain how dolphins can move so expertly. They do not miss when jumping from the water through a hoop. The water does not seem to bother the dolphin's vision. Have you ever opened your eyes under water? If you have, you know it is hard to see much of anything. This is especially true when looking out of the water. Yet the dolphin can hit its mark each time.

The following experiment has been repeated many times at Marineland with the dolphins. It is also meant to test the dolphin's abilities and its vision. Three plywood shapes—a square, a triangle, and a circle—are shown to a dolphin. They are then placed in front of three white panels. Each panel has one of the shapes painted on it in black. The trainer openly places the floating circle in front of the painted circle. All three objects are then thrown into the water. They land about 32 feet (10 m) from the working platform. These objects float, but they lay flat on the water. (This is important to note. This experiment will be repeated later, but with a slight difference to test the dolphin's sonar). At once, the dolphin steers toward the circular float. It takes hold of it and carries it back to the platform. There, the dolphin places it in front of the correct painted panel.

This is done for each object. The dolphin easily completes the task each time. The trainer does not make the slightest gesture of assistance to help the dolphin. There is no trick involved. It is clear that the dolphin's eyesight is good. In fact, it is just as good in the air as in the water. In the water, the dolphin can do without its eyes. Its other senses and its sonar are enough. A dolphin uses its sonar to guide itself and find objects. The dolphin uses its voice to send out sound waves. It then listens for any echoes. From this, the dolphin gathers information about its surroundings.

This sonar system is very effective. It gives the dolphin a much better sense of "sight" under water than its eyes do.

The geometrical shape test always delights people. But to the expert, it is more than a clever trick. It shows a lot about the dolphin's sharp eyesight. It shows even more about its intelligence.

Can dolphins communicate?

Dolphins make a wide range of noises. These include clicks, whistles, clacks, barks, and squawks. The dolphin makes these noises by forcing air through its blowhole. In the air, the sounds can be very loud. Under water, the whistling is much softer and full of strange tones. People sometimes refer to this as the "dolphin's song." Scientists believe that dolphins communicate with each other by making these different sounds. But no one has yet learned to understand this language. It is not clear exactly what the dolphins are "saying."

Scientists have worked with this puzzle for years. Using hydrophones, they have recorded and listened to the dolphin's many sounds. A hydrophone is an instrument for listening to underwater sounds. For years, experts have known that dolphins are intelligent. Because of this, some thought it might be possible for humans and dolphins to communicate. One American scientist, John C. Lilly, spent many years studying this. He did many experiments during the 1950s and 1960s. He did not find an answer. But tests continue even today. Some experts can now separate one dolphin noise from another.

In an interesting meeting, a barking dog draws sharp squeals from the dolphin. Neither animal seems impressed by the noise of the other.

A small girl is drawn to the dolphin pool for a closer look. She talks to the dolphin; it listens. They seem to understand each other.

How intelligent is the dolphin?

The dolphin has an exceptionally well-developed brain. Brighter dolphins have no trouble learning many routines.

The killer whale has a strange shaped head. Its face does not have the dolphin's winning smile. But its brain is more developed than the dolphin's.

No one knows for certain how intelligent dolphins are. But then, intelligence is hard to measure. Should dolphins' thinking be compared with the way people think? Can dolphins think, make decisions, or daydream like people do? Or should they be compared to other animals? In any case, tests show that dolphins do have a kind of intelligence.

The dolphin's brain looks very much like the human brain. At birth, a dolphin's brain is near in size to that of a human baby's. But the dolphin's brain grows much faster. A gifted dolphin quickly learns the exercises it is taught. It has an easy time understanding cause and effect. For example, imagine that a trainer wants the dolphin to come when it hears a whistle. Each time the dolphin obeys, it is given a fish. The dolphin soon understands this. Dolphins also imitate, or copy, each other. When new dolphins come to a zoo, they sometimes learn their routines this way. They pick things up from the zoo's other dolphins.

Because dolphins are intelligent, their behavior can be surprising. Some dolphins will actually show a bad temper. A dolphin may actually sulk in a corner. It may refuse to do any work. Every dolphin has its own nature. This shows in the different reactions each has.

This explains how one dolphin is chosen from the many that are caught. The experts separate the brighter dolphins very quickly. This will bring the best results in the shortest period of time. Sometimes, by mistake, a zoo may end up with a dolphin that is not bright. The zoo directors have paid a lot of money for a loafer. But they will keep the animal. These are the risks of the business.

But are dolphins considered intelligent because they can learn a routine? You may be tempted to say yes. But some routines are still surprising. The following is an example of a routine used at Marineland in France. In this routine, a tiny submarine enters the harbor. It is manned by two divers. The divers pretend to be enemy divers. Their job is to destroy the harbor.

Here is how the operation proceeds:

1. First, the dolphin must find the submarine.
2. The dolphin must swim to the sound buoy.
3. There it presses a lever with its rostrum. It triggers a siren. The base is alerted.
4. The dolphin returns to the submarine. He marks the spot by circling and jumping over it several times.
5. The dolphin returns to the base. Its trainer puts a smoke bomb in its mouth.
6. It sets the bomb near the submarine. The bomb explodes. The submarine sinks.
7. The survivors call for help. The dolphin swims out to them. One of them grabs onto its tail fin.
8. The dolphin brings the diver to the pool's edge.
9. The other diver is busy swimming. The dolphin brings him a

life preserver.

10. The dolphin completes the rescue.

To the dolphins, this is just a routine. But it does not seem this way to the crowd watching it. They do not feel as if they are watching a trained animal. Instead, the dolphin seems an intelligent being.

Another story takes place at Harderwijk Dolphinarium, in the Netherlands. A dolphinarium is a building that houses dolphins. Here, like anywhere else, the dolphins are taught routines. When a dolphin does its routine properly,

it is rewarded with a fish.

But once, the Harderwijk trainer decided to try something new. A dolphin was rewarded only if it did a new exercise. This forced a dolphin to do things that the other dolphins did not know. But as soon as all the dolphins knew the new exercise, the rewards stopped. So the dolphins had to think up new exercises each time. Each new exercise brought a reward. In this case, the dolphins were not performing a routine. This game called for a certain amount of reasoning.

1. Submarine is spotted. 2. First attack.
3. Bomb is placed on the submarine.
4. Bomb goes off. 5. Submarine sinks.
6. Dolphin rescues a survivor. 7. Last man is saved.

What is the dolphin's sonar?

The sounds a dolphin makes are important to its sonar. Scientists believe that the dolphin's sounds begin in its breathing system. They are sent out of the body through an organ called the melon. This fatty organ lies at the top of the animal's head. Here, the melon is shown as a shaded area.

Dolphins use their voices and sharp ears for more than just communicating. According to scientists, they also use these as part of a natural sonar system. A sonar system is a way to find things under water. People have learned to use sonar for many things. Warships and airplanes use it to find enemy ships and submarines. Salvage companies can use sonar to find wrecks. Fishing ships use sonar to locate schools of fish. But bats and dolphins use sonar to guide them.

Sonar is also known as echolocation. This word can be broken into two smaller words: echo and location. Knowing this may help you understand how sonar works. The dolphin's sonar uses *echoes* to *locate* things under water. To do this, the dolphin first sends sound waves into the water. These sound waves are a series of clicks and other noises that the animal makes. They are thought to come from the organ known as the melon. (The melon, you may remember, is an oil deposit found in the dolphin's forehead.) The sound waves will then bounce off of any object they meet. Listening to these echoes, the dolphin gains information about its surroundings. This all seems very simple.

Nature has given the dolphin a very sensitive sonar. It is much more exact than anything that people have created. The dolphin's sonar can do more than just locate things and avoid them. Its brain can also figure an object's shape, its nature, and its distance. The dolphin's sonar can judge all of this. It does not matter whether

A dolphin calmly lets its eyes be covered with rubber suction cups. Apparently, being blindfolded does not frighten the dolphin. Scientists think the dolphin depends more on its sensitive sonar.

Floating shapes are thrown into the water. The dolphin has been told to find the square float. The dolphin quickly finds the objects. After studying them with its sonar, the dolphin chooses the square.

the object is alone or among many other things.

Dolphins "see" everything within their sonar's range in great detail. They locate and avoid things such as rocks, underwater hills, and beaches. Old hulls of ships, floating objects, boats, fishing nets, and even schools of fish are not a problem for the dolphin. With a hydrophone, scientists listen to the dolphins under water. Sometimes, the water is clear and there is nothing unusual in the surroundings. Then the dolphin's sounds are heard only now and then. But in another moment, the conditions change. The water may become murky, or another creature may be nearby. Then the dolphins send out sound waves very rapidly.

Of course, studies have been done in pools with hydrophones. But test results are poor. The pool walls echo the dolphins' sounds. Good recordings are diffi-

cult to get. Some researchers think that the echo does not bother the dolphin. They believe the dolphin gets used to, or adapts to, this echo. After awhile, it pays no attention to it. The animal then learns to use its sonar just as it would in the open sea.

To study the dolphin's sonar, the scientist does experiments. Two examples are found here. In both experiments, the dolphin's eyes were covered with rubber suction cups. These suction cups did not bother the dolphin. Still, experts were surprised that the dolphin allowed its eyes to be covered. Later they understood this. With its powerful sonar, the dolphin does not depend on its eyesight.

In the first test, the trainer showed the dolphin three rubber objects. As in an earlier test, the objects were shaped like a circle, a square, and a triangle. The trainer then pointed to one of the shapes in particular. In this case, it was

the square. After this, the dolphin was blindfolded. All three shapes were tossed into the water. They landed more than 30 feet (10 m) from the animal. The dolphin swam toward them at once. The scientists felt that the dolphin was first guided by its sharp hearing. After that, however, the animal was guided by its sonar. At this point, searching movements of its head were clearly seen. The dolphin quickly found the square, hooked it on its rostrum, and carried it back to its trainer.

The dolphin's sonar also tells the animal much about an object. It can tell, for example, whether an object is soft like a fish, or hard like a stone. The second experiment studied this. For this test, the dolphin was again blindfolded. The trainer then threw both a real fish and a wooden copy of it into the water. At once, the dolphin scooped up the real fish. It totally ignored the wooden double.

What is a marine zoo?

People's admiration for the dolphin did not begin yesterday. This statue, standing in a palace courtyard in Venice, Italy, proves it. Here, a dolphin rolls up at the feet of Neptune. Neptune was the Roman god of the sea. This statue was created by Sansovino in the mid-sixteenth century.

Marine zoos are first of all places of research. But they are also places of entertainment. For the scientist, the zoos are places where the animals can be studied. It would be an impossible thing to try and study dolphins or other marine animals in the wild. Spectators also go to marine zoos to see the animals. But most do not go to study them. Instead, most are drawn by the beauty and excitement of the dolphins. A sense of wonder can be seen on many of their faces.

Marine zoos have given the world much of what it knows about dolphins. They have, in fact, helped create the bond that exists between people and the dolphins. From the outside, these zoos are often similar looking. But in some way, each is different from the rest. Most marine zoos have some special attraction. Often it has something to do with their location. Other times it is in the zoo's purpose or in the animals it holds. Below is a list of some of the most famous marine zoos.

Where are marine zoos in Europe?

Duisburg

The Duisburg Zoo in West Germany is found in the heart of the city. The bleachers for the dolphin pavilion are forever full of school children. The children jump and shout excitedly for the dolphin show. But they are waiting to see the zoo's true stars—a group of belugas.

The zoo's belugas are unique in Europe. These are the large members of the dolphin family. They are known for their strange shaped rostrums. That and their white coloring make them seem unreal. The Duisburg belugas are about 9 to 12 feet (3 to 4 m) long. Their bodies are covered with a thick layer of fat. This layer protects the beluga from the cold arctic waters. The beluga is commonly found in the arctic seas. But it sometimes sneaks into channels nearly closed by ice. Old sailors say that it whistles "like a canary."

Duisburg also boasts a third member of the dolphin family on its grounds. The La Plata dolphin (also known as the Franciscana dolphin) is one of the smallest of all dolphins. Those at the Duisburg Zoo were captured in the brown waters of the Amazon. Three of these grayish brown dolphins are the result of a German expedition. These dolphins have the longest rostrums of any dolphin. Though small, these dolphins seem to be a quarrelsome breed. All three Duisburg dolphins have many scars on their bodies. They obviously fight among themselves.

In the wild, the La Plata dolphins live in muddy, shallow water. During the high water season, they will even move into the

flooded forests. Because of its shallow-water home, the La Plata dolphin has good eyesight. In fact, it has the best eyesight of all freshwater dolphins.

Rapperswil

The Rapperswil Zoo is set on the edge of Zurich Lake in Switzerland. This zoo makes an extra effort to put children and animals in close contact. Here, the dolphin's area is known as the dolphinarium. It is round like a circus ring and can hold a large crowd. Small, black pigs from southeast Asia stroll along the park's walkways. The rhinoceros lets the children gently pet its horn.

Here, dolphins put on a fantastic show. They perform spiral jumps. They walk on their tails, carrying bouquets of flowers in their jaws. They pull children seated in a little boat.

Anvers

The Anvers Zoological Gardens are found in Belgium. At this zoo, the dolphin pool is always buzzing with activity. It is quite different from the zoo's other more peaceful sections.

The Duisburg Zoo in West Germany has a fine collection of marine animals.

The zoo in Rapperswil, Switzerland, offers a show full of many surprises. Here, some young visitors are treated to a boat ride.

29

The belugas, or white whales, are the stars of the Duisburg Zoo. The beluga is known for its strange rostrum and smooth, white coloring. The Duisburg Zoo's belugas are the only belugas in all of Europe.

In recent years the dolphins have become the biggest stars of the zoo. They do three shows per day. Each show fills the hall with people all year round. The dolphin pool has a series of large bay windows running beneath it. From below, visitors can watch the dolphins' underwater play. During the show, people can still watch the dolphins through the windows. The activity of the animals under water is as interesting as the show above the water.

The dolphinarium has seven dolphins. This includes three dolphins of the genus *Sotalia*. These dolphins are small animals living along the coasts of Guyana, Venezuela, and Colombia. They are found in both rivers and seas. Some of them even live in fresh water.

Harderwijk

The largest dolphinarium in Europe is found in the Netherlands. The small village of Harderwijk houses this unique domed theater. The theater seats 2,500 people at a time. From 1965 to 1975, eight million people visited Harderwijk. This is amazing when compared to the country's entire population of thirteen million. From year to year, the zoo's popularity only grows. Germany, to the east, sends tourists by the carload.

Harderwijk's show is well organized and perfectly rehearsed. But the aquarium alone is something to see. The largest in Europe, it is 68 feet (21 m) long and 9 feet (3 m) deep. A dozen dolphins perform in it. They are separated from the people only by a thick glass wall. This setup allows the zoo's visitors to feel a part of the dolphins' world.

A killer whale leaps from the water to catch the fish its trainer throws. Killer whales can be trained much the same as dolphins.

Dolphins can be taught to perform in teams. Here, two dolphins swim backwards at the water's surface. With their powerful tails, they can remain upright while moving.

Where should a visit to the United States begin?

Seaquarium's grounds include a large lagoon. This lagoon is linked directly to the sea. There, three bottle-nosed dolphins perform to music. Three of the zoo's trainers help the dolphins with the routine.

Miami

Miami's Seaquarium is the most famous marine zoo in the world. This is due, in part, to its Florida location. It lies on the edge of Biscayne Bay, in calm waters flooded with sun year round. It covers a total area of 59 acres (24 hectares). The Seaquarium, like most marine zoos, is a place where performance is important. But it is also an important research center. Students from the University of Miami and scientists from all over come to the Seaquarium to study the animals.

Seaquarium was opened in 1955. It even has its own fleet of ships. The ships are used in capturing dolphins from the Caribbean. They are also used in emergencies. A recent example of this happened in the Florida Everglades National Park. A dolphin was carried into the swampy Everglades when a cyclone struck the area. After the storm, the dolphin was trapped in the swamp. The Seaquarium crew was called to help rescue the dolphin. They are often called to help in such cases. Marine animals are often stranded on Florida's gently sloping coasts.

Seaquarium's main pool has six dolphins. All six are very bright and have endless energy. The show is simply put together. Its goal is to highlight the dolphin's skill and power.

Some people may remember the old television series "Flipper." Many episodes of this series were filmed at the Seaquarium. The show's popularity has probably added to the interest in dolphins.

Here you see the killer whale amphitheater in San Diego's Sea World. The Sea World organization has three locations in the United States. Two other Sea Worlds are found in Orlando, Florida, and Aurora, Ohio. The three branches do a huge business. As many as 4,500,000 visitors come through the gates each year.

The killer whale is a feared predator. A predator is an animal that hunts other animals for food. The killer whale is the enemy of all ocean creatures. But it has not been known to attack people.

Where can other dolphin shows be seen in the United States?

Fort Lauderdale

Fort Lauderdale, Florida, is just 9 miles (15 km) from Miami Beach. The city faces the sea and is built around the water. The creation of Ocean World seemed natural there. Ocean World is not the same size as other marine zoos. But the successes of this zoo are the most surprising of any marine zoo.

Six dolphins wait in small, separate pools around the central pool. The demonstration runs for half an hour. Everything moves as if it is run automatically. The routines follow smoothly one after the other. It all looks extremely easy. The trainer interrupts the play only to hand out fish. The

rewards are given sparingly.

The amazing part is that the dolphins perform almost without orders. The trainers do not speak to the dolphins. They use no whistles. They do not give the dolphins any signals or gestures.

Saint Augustine

On Florida's Atlantic coast is Saint Augustine. Saint Augustine is home to Marineland, the oldest of all the oceanariums. It was opened in 1938. Originally, Marineland of Florida was only a research center. The well-known American scientist, Dr. John C. Lilly, began his dolphin studies here. But like many research projects, money was short. Little by

little, the center became a zoo. Once opened to the public, Marineland earned enough money to support itself. It is hard to surpass this center. Its climate, its location, and its design all come together to make Marineland an uncommon success.

Marineland has two demonstration pools. Both offer the usual routines by perfectly trained dolphins. Outside of this, Marineland has a separate aquarium full of interesting creatures. Several kinds of sharks, including a hammerhead shark, live here. Sawfish, manta rays, giant turtles, barracudas, large groupers, moray eels, and an entire range of ocean life are also found here.

Only Sea World presents a living water-skiing routine. Here a trainer rides two bottle-nosed dolphins. Notice how relaxed the skier is. He makes it look simple. Actually, this must have been a very difficult task!

Orlando

Another well-known marine zoo is also found in Florida. This one, known as Sea World, is located in Orlando. Here the show is given more attention than the research. There are two other branches of Sea World found in San Diego, California, and Aurora, Ohio. San Diego's Sea World in California is found near the sea. The location seems to make a difference. San Diego's Sea World is a lot like Miami's Seaquarium.

On command, this dolphin "beaches" itself. In the wild, some dolphins beach themselves to die.

With its three branches, the Sea World organization does a huge business. As many as 4,500,000 visitors come through the gates each year. They pay admission, eat, drink, and spend their money in various gift shops.

But again, the performance seems the important thing here. Sea World offers a spectacular show. Some of the routines seem nearly impossible. An example of this is water-skiing on the back of two dolphins. The dolphins go along with this routine without any objection. It is a fine example of the dolphins' training.

The opening to the sea can be seen at the far left of this photo. The dolphins are free to swim in the open water. Some explore it, but usually not for very long.

Flipper's Sea School is a genuine school for dolphins. In its simple setting, the school selects and trains bright dolphins for use in marine zoos. At the school, the dolphins learn very basic exercises. Later, more complicated routines will be built upon these. The school is important in that it gives a dolphin its earliest training. At this stage, it learns to respond to a trainer. This single thing is the key to the entire training process.

A trainer and her student share a quiet moment.

Is there a school for dolphins?

Flipper's Sea School is the only school for dolphins in the world. It is located near Key Largo, Florida. At first glance, Flipper's Sea School is somewhat rustic. This is especially true compared to Seaquarium.

Here, no one cares about appearances. Results are the most important thing. The different pools and enclosures are separated by wooden posts. They are closed off from the sea by a simple rock dike. There, gray pelicans perch. The pools house only a few dolphins at a time. All are undergoing training.

Among these dolphins are two large males. They, like the others, are free to go into the sea. An opening into the sea allows them to make small trips into the open water. But these trips never last very long. Perhaps the dolphins get bored when they are alone in these vast waters. Perhaps they are not sure how to find food. The school is just a few jumps away. There they have all the comforts of home.

Flipper's Sea School is defined as a school for training dolphins. Mainly, the school's staff selects bright dolphins for training. They then teach the dolphin students a few basic exercises. The school encourages close contact between trainers and dolphins. Training a dolphin depends on this. Some exercises are hard even for the agile dolphins. Some actions are not normal, or natural, for a dolphin to do. These exercises call for much patience.

After this, the dolphins are sold to other marine zoos. These zoos build on the training begun at Flipper's Sea School. But the basic training is done by the school's experts.

A dolphin and its trainer play ball. Dolphins are very skilled at using their rostrums for different activities.

How do the zoos care for the dolphins?

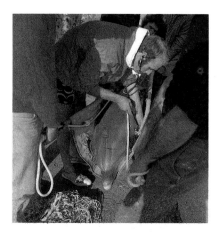

The staff of a marine zoo spares no effort when animals get sick. It takes gigantic efforts when a killer whale is sick. At Marineland of Antibes, the staff once even put an oxygen tent over the entire pool.

A sick dolphin needs a great amount of care. Sometimes this means watching the animal around the clock.

Zoo staffs take very good care of their dolphins. An animal's health is given constant attention. Veterinarians give the animals regular check-ups. The animals are given any vitamins or medicines they need. Still, even dolphins get sick sometimes. As soon as a dolphin shows any signs of being sick, samples are taken from its blowhole. Blood tests then show what the treatment should be.

Dolphins are given the same medicines that people take. But dolphins are much bigger than people. They may need larger amounts of a medicine. The doctor considers this weight difference when caring for the dolphins.

But examining a dolphin can be difficult. For example, taking a blood sample from a dolphin is not easy. There are two solutions to this problem. One is to empty the pool in which the dolphin lives. Then the animal is stranded on a dry surface. However, this takes a lot of time. It is an impossible method if blood samples are needed often. A doctor will sometimes need samples every day. This is one way to keep a close watch on the patient. A doctor will do this if the dolphin has been given a new drug or is not getting any better.

The other method is to catch the dolphin with a net and take it from the pool. This method is faster, but more people are needed to do it.

What are killer whales really like?

The killer whale is a beautiful member of the dolphin family. It is ferocious in the wild. It is sometimes called "sea-tiger." The killer whale is easily recognized by its black back and white underside. It is also 16 to 29 feet (5 to 9 m) long and weighs three to five tons. Its tail fin is well developed and very powerful. The dorsal fin can be as large as 5 feet (1.80 m) high in the largest males. A fin that curves and falls over is often a sign of illness.

The killer whale also has a huge mouth with forty to forty-eight sharp teeth. The teeth can be up to 3 inches (8 cm) long. They are used to catch and hold prey. The whale's very small eyes are almost invisible. They easily blend in with its black skin.

Killer whales feed mainly on fish. They will sometimes attack other animals such as seals, walruses, and dolphins. Dolphins as long as 9 feet (3 m) have been found in the whale's stomach. The whale sometimes travels in groups. In groups of ten to twenty, the killer whale can even attack larger whales. It has not been known to attack people.

Many people come to Sea World to see the killer whales. Amphitheaters there hold three to four thousand people. One whale in particular attracts the crowds. It is the famous killer whale, Shamu. One of the unique routines at Sea World includes trick riding. For this stunt, Shamu's trainer rides on the whale's back. Together, whale and rider complete a series of dives.

But people have not always

been so easy around the killer whales. An ancient drawing in Peru shows the killer whale's thirst for blood. Indeed, the outline of a killer whale can be seen near the village of El Ingenio. The outline can only be seen from the air. It shows one of these mighty animals holding a man's head in its jaws. This suggests that the ancient fishermen may have had run-ins with the whale. Even today, fishermen in Iceland must deal with killer whales. Sometimes the killer whales attack the fishermen's nets.

San Diego's Sea World show includes trick riding as seen here. This stunt is unique in all the world. Three times, Shamu dives under the water. Each time the whale's tiny rider holds onto it with a hoop. The exercise is a dangerous one. The rider carries an oxygen tank in case of a problem.

How does the killer whale behave in captivity?

Killer whales are gentle in captivity. Like dolphins, they can easily be trained. With killer whales, however, extra care must be taken. These animals can be 16 to 29 feet (5 to 9 m) long. They often weigh from 3 to 5 tons.

For many years, the killer whale was seen as a feared predator. Fishermen hated the whale and killed it on sight. In fact, hunting killer whales was allowed in many countries. People felt they were a threat to other marine animals and the fishing trade. People saw little good in the animal.

In 1961, a killer whale was captured alive for the first time. It was taken to a marine zoo. There it lived only a little while. But after this, people's thinking began to change. A few years later, a killer whale was trapped in a fishing net. It was sold to the owner of the Seattle Public Aquarium. The whale, later called Namu, was very bright. It was friendly, agreeable, and responded to training. Its trainers hand-fed it, played with it, and swam with it. They even rode on its back. Namu changed the killer whale's reputation forever.

Today, there are many killer whales in marine zoos around the world. Many are found to be very gentle and agreeable in captivity. In short, they are said to act like big dolphins. Like dolphins, they play games, learn routines, and enjoy contact with people. Many experts think that the killer whale is as bright as, or brighter than, the dolphin.

But, nevertheless, the trainers must be very careful. Because of its size, the killer whale can be dangerous even when playing. In one example, a whale rider was grabbed by the leg and dragged about the pool. This was not thought to be a hostile act. If the whale had meant to kill the rider, it easily could have.

How do killer whales attack?

Groups of killer whales will sometimes attack a school of dolphins. But this attack calls for a special approach. Several of the whales begin by very quickly circling the dolphins. At the right moment an attacker pounces on a victim. The killer whale takes only one bite . . . and leaves the rest for the next one. The circling then starts all over again.

This method is also good for hunting seals. In the warm season, the ice begins to break up. Small islands of ice drift away, carrying sunbathing seals with them. Along comes a killer whale. Killer whales are always hungry.

With one stroke of its tail, the whale leaps from the water. It throws half of its weight onto the ice block. The block of ice tips under the weight. The seal slides into the predator's mouth. Killer whales may have attacked people the same way.

In his diary, English explorer Robert F. Scott describes such an attack. Scott was the first person to reach the South Polar plateau. This account comes from a later expedition, on January 5, 1911. At the time, Scott's ship was encircled in ice. A group of killer whales passed beneath the ice. They swam to a section on which a photographer and two sled dogs were stranded. They pushed up the ice. It broke with a great noise. Then the killer whales threw themselves against the ice pieces. Luckily, the man and the dogs kept their balance. The whales, bobbing in the water, seemed surprised by their failure. They finally left with nothing to show for their efforts.

It is easy to see, then, why the area empties out when the whales arrive. Luckily, it is also easy to know when they are near. Killer whales on patrol exchange whistling sounds. Many animals know this sound and flee.

How are dolphins trained?

It could be said that dolphin training is based on a mutual relationship. That is, the trainer and the dolphin both give something, and both get something. In a way, that is true. For the trainer's part, it is, "I will give you a fish, if you work for me." For the dolphin it is, "I will work for you, if you give me a fish." This agreement makes everyone happy.

The words tamer, instructor, and trainer are all used to describe the person who trains the dolphin. These words suggest that the person involved is in control of the animal. More often, it is the

other way around. The instructor or trainer must count on the dolphin's cooperation. Some people wonder whether it is the dolphin who does the training.

Training a dolphin calls for much patience. A bright, willing dolphin can learn several exercises in a very short period of time. But some dolphins are simply untrainable. Some of these animals simply do not want to be trained. Others truly are not able to learn.

Then, of course, dolphins, like any other animals, can be disagreeable sometimes. There are

many reports of dolphins sulking in corners. Sometimes an animal may refuse to come from its cage. In either case, there is little the trainer can do. It is pointless to work with the animal then.

Punishment is never used in training a dolphin. This will only make the dolphin less willing. Positive rewards work best. Often, the dolphin will willingly do what it is asked. Many dolphins are eager to please their trainers. Others seem to take great pleasure in just performing. These animals need little encouragement.

How important is the dolphin's play?

Many kinds of animals love to play. Cats play with yarn. Dogs chase their tails. You have probably seen lion cubs or young monkeys rolling and tumbling together at the zoo or in a film. It is not uncommon to see.

Dolphins also play. It is a very important part of their lives. But dolphins' play is different than that of many animals. Dolphins' play is organized. Often an entire school will participate in a game.

Dolphins' play shows an ability to observe and copy. Some people say that it also shows imagination and an inventive spirit. Some see it as evidence of the dolphin's intelligence.

Dolphins seem to find fun in everything. Performing for people seems to please them. But playing among themselves is also important. Dolphins will spend hours playing with a ball, a floating ring, or anything nearby. But the dolphin will also create its own entertainment. The dolphinologist (one who studies dolphins) John Lilly tells of one game created by three dolphins. The game was begun in the middle of a training session. The trainer, Ken, was trying to get the dolphins to jump through a hoop. He was holding a fish at its other side as a reward. The first dolphin made a dive toward the hoop. At the same time, another dolphin came up behind Ken and snatched the fish. The third dolphin then rushed between Ken's legs, making him lose his balance. The dolphins repeated the game for the entire session.

Scientists do not think that captive dolphins' play comes from boredom. It is also not a result of training. Dolphins in the wild play just as much. In part, the play results from the dolphins' need for contact. Dolphins are very social animals. That is, they need to be with others. Scientists have seen this in their research. A dolphin is not happy when it is alone. It gets bored easily and grows weak. When that same dolphin is put with other dolphins, it acts very differently. It soon recovers its playfulness and spirit.

When fed in the water, the dolphin tends to jump after fish. This is the way it eats in the wild.

Can a friendship exist between a dolphin and its trainer?

But, when fed near the work platform, the dolphin is gentle. It calmly reaches up to accept the food. These two photos show very different actions.

The trainer's contact with the dolphin is very important. Dolphins are very sensitive to gentle touches and soft words. With them, a trainer will soon win a dolphin's trust and friendship. The animal-trainer relationship is the key to a dolphin's training. This is especially true at the beginning. A strong bond will bring out the best in a dolphin. But the instructor must respect this bond. It must never be abused. Otherwise, the dolphin will refuse to do anything for the trainer. It will go on a "work-strike."

There are only a few ways of showing displeasure to the dolphin. The trainer can refuse to give the fish reward, turn away from the dolphin, or leave the work area. This last possibility is only for extreme cases. This sounds silly. But it works very often with dolphins and even with killer whales. And killer whales are not known to be overly sensitive.

So, people and animals work together on an equal footing. The dolphin willingly takes the trainer's orders. Yet it has the freedom to refuse. It may do this when it is bored, distracted, or not feeling well. Under these conditions, the reward will not work in any way.

Does the dolphin obey the trainer's whistle?

Even in the strangest positions, the whistle is important. The whistle is the main form of communication between dolphin and instructor. The dolphin learns this code quickly. It greatly speeds up the training. Both trainer and dolphin are interested in learning quickly.

From the start, the dolphin trainer uses a whistle. As each fish is taken, the whistle is blown. This is a means of communication between dolphin and trainer. The whistle is blown with all commands, all calls to order, and with any correct actions. The dolphin soon learns a code for good or bad conduct. This is part of the dolphin-instructor relationship from the start.

A sample of this language goes as follows:
—one long blow for "Yes,"
—several blows in a row: "Yes, that's good, go on,"
—one short blow: "Stop,"
—a series of short blows: "No, come back here,"
—two powerful blows in a row: "No, let's start over."

This simple whistle language is made of five words or expressions. With these few commands, a trainer can organize a complete show. It is truly hard to believe.

A few gestures are learned along with the whistle. The gestures used are always the same. They are kept as short and as meaningful as possible. They will help the new dolphin quickly understand what is expected of it. Once an exercise has been learned, the dolphin's memory will do the rest. Just presenting the object used: a ball, a pole, a bowling pin, rings, or a surfboard will trigger the dolphin's reaction. But the visitor is often fooled by the apparent ease of the performance.

The dolphin's memory is also jogged by the music from the show. The tune that begins the show excites the dolphins waiting in the pool. In many ways, it serves as a warm-up.

The dolphin trainers have no secret practices. The only thing that counts is know-how. It comes, in part, from experience. But it also comes from the trainer's understanding of the dolphins. With this understanding, a trainer can almost predict an animal's reactions.

How does a trainer teach the dolphin its routines?

This dolphin has learned to bowl as part of its routine. The trainer's gestures help the dolphin direct the ball. With them, the trainer can adjust the dolphin's position to within a few inches (centimeters).

Teaching a dolphin a routine is a long process. Imagine trying to teach a dolphin to jump over a high pole. It may seem easy. It is . . . after it has been learned. But, in the ocean, a dolphin rarely deals with obstacles. There aren't any. If by chance one pops up, there is plenty of room. It would be easy to avoid.

So, the trainer begins by asking the dolphin to jump over a pole held at the water's surface. At first, the dolphin is not willing.

But soon, the dolphin approaches the pole to study the strange object. Then, seeing it as a chance for play, the dolphin jumps the pole. The whistle blows, the fish is given. The training process has begun.

Of course, things do not always go so fast. It may take several hours or days for this first jump. Then, little by little, the pole is set higher and higher. Finally, the dolphin arrives at the set goal. But it takes time. Of course, if the dolphin is cooperative, it goes faster. But the trainer must always be patient. There will be problems to face each day. Some days the dolphin will refuse to cooperate. On other days, the routines will not work. Of course, there will always be things to distract the dolphin.

But once a dolphin learns something, it is learned for good. This is what is important. Another common dolphin routine is football, or tailball, in dolphin language. This game calls for a different approach. The hard part is getting the dolphin to lie on its back. The dolphin must lie in front of the platform within the trainer's reach. Then, with a short whistle, the trainer taps lightly on the dolphin's tail. The dolphin quickly picks this up. Soon it taps the trainer's hand with each whistle. Then the trainer adds a ball, holding it as the dolphin taps it. The whistle is blown. This is repeated many times. Finally, the trainer lets go of the ball. With a tap, the dolphin sends it flying into the air. The whistle is blown and the fish is given.

After several tries, the trainer simply throws the ball into the middle of the pool. The dolphin dashes out to it. Quickly, it rolls onto its back under the ball. With a powerful slap of its tail, the dolphin sends it high into the air. Before long, the dolphin plays this with other dolphins.

The full somersault is one of the most amazing exercises. But even dolphins in the wild do this. Sailors have seen dolphins do this at sea. But now the dolphin must do this on command. Often this exercise is learned by chance. One day, in tossing the ball, the dolphin does a complete flip. The whistle is blown in approval. The dolphin is given a double reward. The exercise is repeated many times. Before long the dolphin will perform the somersault on command.

Three dolphins jump a tightrope as a team. Team acts are even more difficult. They require perfect timing and cooperation from all the dolphins. These dolphins are part of the show at Fort Lauderdale's Ocean World (Florida).

Teaching a dolphin to play football is time-consuming at first. Before long, however, the dolphin is making powerful shots. It shoots the ball to a height of 49 feet (15 m). The ball often ends up in the grandstands.

How is the dolphin taught to jump through a hoop?

Making a dolphin jump through a hoop is not so easy. Dolphins are frightened when they are suddenly surrounded by solid objects. This does not happen at sea unless a dolphin is caught in a net. But then it is too shocked to resist. To the dolphin, the hoop is a solid object. The trainer must teach the dolphin not to be afraid of it.

To begin, the trainer lays the hoop on the water's surface. The dolphin examines it cautiously, circling around it. With a gesture, the trainer invites the dolphin to go through the hoop. For some dolphins, this may work at once. For others it may take hours, or even several days.

In the first case, the dolphin willingly goes through the hoop. This simple act is repeated many times. Soon, the dolphin loses its fear. Only then will the trainer raise the hoop. At this point, the trainer must follow two rules. First, the hoop must always be held in the same spot. Second, the dolphin must not accidentally knock against the hoop. Both of these rules are very important. If either rule is broken, the dolphin will be frightened. The trainer will then have to start all over.

The show can be made more exciting by setting fire to the hoop. Dolphins know nothing of fire. They have good reason to be frightened of it and refuse to work. The trainer would have no way of forcing the dolphin into it in this case. Yet often, dolphins willingly obey. This shows that the dolphin puts great trust in its trainer. You can see why the relationship between them is so important.

This part of the exercise must be taught very slowly. The trainer begins by setting fire to a small part of the hoop. The dolphin jumps once, then ten times. Finally, it gains confidence. Before long, the fire seems unimportant. Because the dolphin jumps quickly, the fire does not hurt it.

The dolphin dance looks like an easy exercise. Actually, it takes a lot of strength. At Sea World in Orlando, two dolphins dance in circles to the rhythm of a waltz.

How do dolphins live at sea?

At sea, dolphins live in groups. The groups may include from six to several hundred dolphins. They are often led by an important and respected leader. Even in captivity there is usually a leader. As soon as a group has formed, a leader appears very quickly. It is also thought that there are dominant dolphins within a group. Because certain dolphins are dominant, the group then has an order. This has also been seen in captive dolphins.

Dolphins living in groups take care of each other. The females help each other look after the young. You have already seen that they help each other give birth. But dolphins of both sexes seem to be protective. Again, this is partly because dolphins are social animals. They enjoy living in groups and depend on each other for survival.

Scientists have studied these groups for years. Now and then, they are rewarded with amazing sights. Jacques-Yves Cousteau tells of such a sight in his book *Dolphins and Freedom*. He writes:

"On the other side of the island, we spotted a dolphin which was coming up to breathe and was letting itself sink without appearing to swim. We approached silently and got into the water. What we then saw we were never to see again. There were about fifteen dolphins, it was probably

the school that we had seen go by regularly. These dolphins were in 32 to 39 feet (10 to 12 m) of crystal clear water, on the side of the reef. They seemed to be sitting on the bottom in a group as if they were holding a meeting. They were literally resting on their tails, they did not move off.

We saw them turn their heads toward us. We were on the surface, and had no diving suits. At first they stayed motionless, then moved around. They continued to hold their meeting and it was quite a sight. When we tried to get closer to them, they left. It was a unique, wonderful sight."

A dolphin jumps through a flaming hoop at the Anvers Zoo in Belgium. Once the dolphin has learned this, many things are possible. Such jumps can be made at all heights. One, two, three, or even four dolphins can jump at once. They can even jump in opposite directions.

Does the dolphin have enemies?

The dolphin is a gentle and friendly animal. But that does not mean that it does not have enemies. It does. The worst of all the dolphin's enemies is the killer whale. But there is also the shark. All of these animals live in the same waters of the world. They can't help meeting. What happens when they meet depends on which animal is stronger at the time.

In a group, dolphins are not afraid of anything. They are excellent fighters if they have to be. This is because they always attack in a group. This gives them an advantage over the shark, which fights alone. Now and then, an overly brave shark attacks a school of dolphins. Such a shark does not survive the counterattack. The dolphins quickly dive under the shark. They use their rostrums to strike the soft part of its belly. Their rostrums are as hard as cement. They can cause a shark's liver to burst. Under these conditions a smart shark will run away.

The dolphin's rostrum is amazingly strong. Its strength comes from its ability to lock its jaws. This is helped by the fact that its

At first sight, the dolphin's rostrum does not seem like much of a weapon. But it is as hard as cement. It works so well that most sharks would rather run than face it.

teeth interlock. This makes the jaw very rigid. When it hits, the shock shoots down the dolphin's spine. The full weight of its body follows it. The dolphin's strong tail adds to its defense. With it, the dolphin can charge with great speed and force.

So, it seems that the dolphin is very able to defend itself. But still, the dolphin should be on guard! If it wanders off from the group, it could find trouble. A lone dolphin is not so much of a threat. A 12 foot (4 m) long "blue skin" shark will be able to overpower it.

In aquariums, dolphins and sharks can live together without any problem. But if a dolphin is about to give birth, they must be separated. Blood in the water at-tracts the shark. Even in an aquarium, this could be dangerous.

Dolphins have a reputation as shark fighters. One story involves a Soviet ship off the Kamchatka Peninsula. The crew suddenly heard loud roaring. It turned out to be a sea lion surrounded by sharks. Two minutes later, a group of dolphins arrived. They chased the sharks away. Later, the dolphins returned to check on the sea lion. The sharks had also returned. This time, they chased the sharks off once and for all.

Dolphins, seals, and sea lions seem to get along well. This "friendship" is often noticed in marine zoos. There these warm-blooded animals are in close contact.

The aquarium of Marineland in Florida has many species of sharks. Even in captivity, the shark is a frightening creature.

Aren't people the dolphin's worst enemies?

In some cases, people are the dolphin's worst enemies. They kill hundreds of thousands of tons of cetaceans each year. Many of these are killed for commercial uses. Dolphin meat is used in canned pet food. Others use the fat and oil from the animal's body. Still other dolphins are killed by fishermen. Local fishermen some-times accuse the dolphin of dis-rupting the good fishing spots.

But one of the greatest of dangers to dolphins is the tuna fisher-men. The tuna fishermen are not hunting dolphins. They are hunt-ing tuna. But for some reason, schools of tuna are often found swimming near schools of dol-phins. The tuna seem to follow the dolphins, relying on their good sense of direction. When the tuna fish are netted, many dolphins get caught, too. Tens of thousands of dolphins die this way each year.

Laws now protect the dolphin in the United States. The tuna fishermen have been ordered to find new fishing methods. These methods must allow the dolphins to escape from the nets. It may take some time to find such meth-ods. In the meantime, the fisher-men must separate the dolphins from the tuna. The dolphins must be set free, unharmed. The fishing fleets must cooperate or be shut down. This makes the fishermen's job more difficult. It requires much more time and work. Sometimes fishermen must dive into these masses to pull the dolphins out. This can be a very risky job.

Similar protective measures have been started just about every-where. People now see the impor-tance of these measures. Protect-ing nature has become more and more a part of people's thinking. In the Black Sea and the Mediter-ranean, hunting is now forbid-den. Some Antilles fishermen still find it necessary to eat dolphins. But they will not empty the ocean by chasing the dolphins. They hunt the dolphins in small motor-ized fishing boats using harpoon guns.

More people are now aware of the dolphins' problems. Many of them are making an effort to help protect these animals. Marine zoos are very much a part of this effort. Their activities keep people in-formed.

How have dolphins been taught to protect people?

The dolphin lifeguard has spotted a shark swimming in the area. Immediately, the dolphin turns on a siren. The siren alerts the swimmers of the possible danger. The dolphin then attacks the shark to make it leave.

Dolphins' natural dislike of sharks has led to interesting experiments. Experts have trained some dolphins to protect swimmers against shark attacks. This idea is already used experimentally in Port Elizabeth, South Africa. Shark attacks happen very often in the Indian Ocean. Many public beaches are already protected by nets.

The show at Marineland of Antibes includes a small example of this training. It is simply designed, but it does have one problem. It

teaches the normally peaceful dolphin to attack.

For the routine, a plastic shark is thrown into the water. The dolphin rushes at once to a floating siren. Such a siren could be anchored in the water near a beach. The dolphin uses its rostrum to trigger the siren. After that, the dolphin rushes back to the shark. With a powerful blow, the dolphin sends the shark dummy flying into the air.

One dolphin trained for this has already been put on duty on a Florida beach. In the future, more dolphins may be added to this shark patrol. This could someday be very useful in areas where sharks are often found.

How long have people and dolphins been friends?

There are many stories about dolphins in ancient legends. Potters, sculptors, and painters used the dolphin's image in their work. The dolphin decorates many ancient vases, plates, drawings, sculptures, and other artworks. Oddly, the common dolphin seemed to be better known two thousand years ago than it is now. Were meetings with dolphins more frequent? Were there more dolphins? In any event, this strange friendship is definitely ancient. It was perhaps even more common than it is today.

Stories of this friendship come from the Roman scholar, Pliny, the Elder. Pliny, who was also a writer, lived around 70 A.D. According to Pliny, relationships much like friendships existed between children and dolphins. Thus, "for it (the dolphin), man is no stranger." As evidence, Pliny gives three examples.

In the first, Pliny tells of a dolphin who lived in Lake Lucrino. This dolphin made friends with a boy, the son of a poor man. On his way to school, the boy stopped to feed the dolphin. Each morning, he would stand at the shore and call the dolphin. The dolphin always came quickly. When it had received its treat, the dolphin would carry the child across the lake to school. Each afternoon, the dolphin would carry the boy back the same way. The story says

This ancient mosaic comes from the floor of the Roman villa "del Casale." A mosaic is a picture or pattern made with small pieces of different colored material. This mosaic shows a child swimming with dolphins.

that one day the child did not come. He had died during the night. The dolphin was unable to stand the disappearance of its friend. It died of a broken heart.

The second story is very strange. It tells of a dolphin and a child named Iassus. The dolphin was known to be very fond of Iassus. One day the dolphin followed the child back into the shallow water. Eagerly, it tried to follow him back onto the land. The dolphin accidentally stranded itself on the sand and died.

The last story is no less strange. It tells of another child, who traveled the seas on a dolphin's back. The child, named Hermias, was killed by a sudden storm. When he was brought back dead, the dolphin blamed itself. It did not return to the sea, but let itself die on the sand.

As you can see by the stories, ancient people respected the dol-

This statuette from the Museum of Palermo shows a man riding a dolphin. It is Greek. Its dolphins look much more realistic than the Roman dolphins. The Roman artists often decorated their dolphins. Some artists gave them extra scales or tail fins divided into three parts.

phins. They considered the dolphins as beings very close to people. Some people even thought that dolphins were people changed into sea animals. There are many legends.

A more recent story is told by a sailor named Bernard Moitessier. Moitessier was saved by dolphins during his last trip around the world. His boat had changed di-

Dolphins are often seen playing around ships at sea. They seem to enjoy swimming just in front of a boat's bow. Here a group of dolphins plays near the bow, fascinating a dog on board.

rection in the fog without his knowledge. It was headed straight onto unmarked reefs. Moitessier's story makes an interesting adventure. He retells it in his book *The Long Road*. Here are some parts from it:

"I hear familiar whistles. I go out quickly, as I always do when the dolphins are here. But I do not believe I have ever seen so many. Their splashing makes the water white, furrowed in all directions by their knife-like dorsal fins. There are nearly a hundred of them. A tight line of twenty-five dolphins swims from the rear to the front of the boat, on the starboard side, in three breaths. Then the whole group speeds ninety degrees to the right, all the dorsal

fins cutting the water together in a single motion in flight.

They repeat the same thing more than ten times. Never had I seen such a perfectly orchestrated ballet. And they always rush to the right, whitening the sea for about thirty meters. They are obeying an exact command, but I do not know whether it is always the same group of twenty to twenty-five; there are too many dolphins to be able to recognize them. They seem nervous. I do not understand. The others look nervous too, and swim in a zig-zag path with a great deal of splashing, frequently slapping the water with their tails, instead of playing near the bow as they ordinarily do. The whole sea whistles with their cries.

Another passage from back to front with this same quick turning to the right. What are they playing today? I have never seen this . . . . Why are they nervous? They are nervous, that I am sure of. And I had never seen that either.

Something pulls at me, I look at the compass. . . . *Joshua* [the boat] is running with the wind behind it . . . right onto Steward Island, hidden in the fog. The strong wind from the west has turned south without my realizing it. I did not detect the change in course because of the rather calm sea . . .

I lower the staysail, then plank the sheets and adjust the weather vane for the close haul. We certainly are more than fifty miles from the outlying rocks which border Stewart Island. But how long was *Joshua* heading for the coast hidden in the fog? Was it just before the first passage of the dolphins with their ninety degree turn to the right . . . Or well before their arrival, even before their first display?

I climb back on the bridge, after taking a few puffs of my cigarette. There are just as many of them as before. But now they are playing with *Joshua*, in a fan shape in front and in a line on the sides, with the gay movements I have always known dolphins to make.

And this is when I see the most amazing thing: a large black and white dolphin jumps three or four meters (9 - 12 feet) high in an amazing somersault, with two complete turns. And it lands flat, with its tail forward.

Whenever a ship nears a school of dolphins, they always show themselves. With great speed, some of the dolphins race around the ship. Others play in its wake. This often lasts several minutes. In the case of Bernard Moitessier, however, the dolphins stayed several hours.

Three times in a row it repeats this double somersault, from which it derives enormous joy. You could say that it is crying to me and the other dolphins: 'The man has understood that we were telling him to go right! . . . You have understood . . . you have understood! . . . Continue like that, everything is clear straight ahead! . . .'

Standing with my oilskin, my hood, my boots and my leather gloves, I hold a stay of the large mast to the wind. Almost all my dolphins are now swimming on the windward side, too. That surprises me a bit more. Sometimes they turn onto their sides. Their left eye can be clearly seen. I believe that they are looking at me. They must be able to see me very well, thanks to the yellow oilskin which stands out against the white of the sails and the red hull.

My dolphins have been swimming around *Joshua* for more than two hours. The dolphins that I had encountered before

Here a dolphin goes through a life-
saving routine. It tows its trainer
through the water to safety.

rarely played for more than about fifteen minutes before continuing on their way. But these will stay for more than two hours all in all. When they left, two of them stayed near me until dusk, a total of five full hours. They swim, one on the right and the other on the left, looking slightly bored.

They have been swimming like that for three hours, one on each side, adjusting their speed to the speed of *Joshua,* without playing, two or three meters from the boat. I have never seen that before. Never have I been accompanied so long by dolphins. I am sure that they had received orders to stay near me until *Joshua* was absolutely out of danger."

The Irish setter has plenty of nerve. It competes with the killer whale for the fish their trainer throws.

Despite the dolphin's large size, many animals are not frightened by it. Here a dolphin offers a fish to a cat. Even up close, the cat does not seem nervous.

In a quiet moment, a killer whale and its trainer enjoy a swim around the pool. Although communication between them may be limited, it seems no problem here.

What does the future hold for the dolphin?

People are learning more about dolphins every day. Dolphins are very interesting because they are not like any other animals. To this day, experts have many unanswered questions. Some of these questions have excited the wildest of dreams. But one thing is for certain. The more people learn about dolphins, the more special they become.

In the future, dolphins will no doubt become more important to people. Certainly they will play a part in the exploration of the oceans. The exploration of the seas has hardly begun. Perhaps the dolphin will be an important aid for all tasks waiting there. This is certainly possible. The dolphin is an extremely gifted, if not "rational" being. At the very least, they can be trained. They can assist with many tasks already. So people will no doubt continue to use them. But these tasks will not bother the dolphin. The dolphin considers most things play. . . . Still, the animal must be respected and treated with affection.

The military has attempted some experiments already. Some of these experiments involved more marine animals than just dolphins. Killer whales and sea lions were also used. These animals were trained to act as messengers, tool carriers, and scouts. But not very much is known about these tests.

Ancient myths have predicted what the dolphin could represent in the future. Did not the ancient people speak of the "language" of the dolphin? But 2,500 years later, people are still only beginning to understand it.

Friendships between dolphins and people can begin at any age. Some people suggest that contact between children and dolphins should be encouraged. Such experiments would be possible in warm climates.

The dolphin is truly a friendly animal. As seen throughout this book, it needs the company of others to be happy. A good trainer can make the most of this need. A dolphin is often just as happy being with people as it is with another dolphin.

Glossary

adapt to adjust to new environments or situations.

baleen the hundreds of tiny plates found in the mouth of a baleen whale. These thin plates hang from the whale's upper jaw. The whale uses its baleen to filter food from the water. It is made of the same substance as human fingernails.

baleen whales one of the two major groups of the cetacean order. Baleen whales have no teeth. Instead they use their filter-like mouths to strain plankton from the water.

beaching a tendency among marine animals to drive themselves up onto land. Dolphins and other cetaceans will beach, or strand, themselves when they are sick, injured, or ready to die.

bends a painful condition that is caused by nitrogen gas bubbles in the bloodstream and body tissues. This happens when the air pressure surrounding the body is lowered too quickly. Scuba divers sometimes experience the bends when they surface too quickly.

blowhole an opening at the top of a cetacean's head. The blowhole is connected to the animal's air passages. It is used for breathing and for producing sounds.

blubber a layer of fat found in many cetaceans which serves to insulate the animal and maintain its body temperature.

bottle-nosed dolphin one of the two most common kinds of dolphins. This dolphin, also known as *Tursiops truncatus* is found in all oceans. It is thought to be one of the most intelligent of all animals. For this reason, it is often the bottle-nosed dolphin that is seen performing in zoos and aquariums.

caudal fin another name for the dolphin's flukes (*see* fluke).

cetacean an order of aquatic mammals including dolphins, whales, porpoises, etc. Cetaceans have large heads plus fish-like, hairless bodies, and flippers for front limbs. The cetacean's body tapers to a powerful tail with which the animal propels itself.

common dolphin one of the two most common kinds of dolphins. The common dolphin, or *Delphinus delphis,* is found in warm ocean waters throughout the world. This dolphin has a black body, a white underside, and distinct yellowish stripes on its flanks. The common dolphin does not do as well in captivity as the bottle-nosed dolphin.

crustacean any of a large class of animals whose bodies are protected by hard, shell-like coverings. Lobsters, shrimp, and crabs are crustaceans.

Delphinus delphis (*see* common dolphin).

dolphin fish a large game fish that lives in warm salt waters.

dorsal fin the dolphin's back fin. The dorsal fin is important to the animal's steering and balance.

drag the slowing force acting on any body moving through a fluid. This force is opposite to the direction of the body's motion.

echolocation a dolphin's natural sonar system with which it locates objects under the water. Through echolocation, the dolphin sends out sound waves. These are reflected back by any solid objects they encounter. Listening to the echoes, the dolphin gathers information about its surroundings.

environment the forces and conditions by which one is surrounded. An environment consists of physical, chemical, and biotic factors. An animal's environment, for example, includes such factors as climate, food supply, and other animals. These factors act upon an animal and ultimately determine its form and survival.

flukes powerful tail fins such as those of the dolphin and whale. Unlike fish which have vertical tails, the cetacean's flukes are horizontal. Moving them in an up and down motion, the animal propels itself quickly through the water.

hydrophone an instrument for listening to sounds transmitted through water.

melon a fatty oil deposit found in the dolphin's head. The melon causes the dolphin's characteristic bulging forehead. The dolphin uses the melon in echolocation.

pectoral fin either of the front fins of an aquatic animal, such as a fish or a cetacean. The dolphin's pectoral fins are sometimes called flippers.

plankton drifting masses of minute animal and plant life in a body of water. Baleen whales commonly feed on plankton.

pod a number of animals clustered together. Whales often travel in huge groups known as pods.

rostrum a dolphin's beak.

school a large number of animals of one kind swimming together. Groups of dolphins and fish are often called schools.

social animals animals that live together and depend on each other for survival.

species a group of animals which scientists have identified as having common traits.

toothed whales one of the two main groups of the cetacean order. Unlike the baleen whales, toothed whales have teeth. But they use their teeth only to capture their prey, not to chew it. Toothed whales swallow their food whole. Dolphins are grouped with the toothed whales because of their similar body features.

Tursiops truncatus (*see* bottle-nosed dolphin).

warm-blooded having a high body temperature which remains about the same despite the temperature of the surroundings. Whales and dolphins, like all mammals, are warm-blooded.

INDEX